INK OF FEELINGS

ANMOL RAI SAMSUHANG

Made with ♥ on the Notion Press Platform
www.notionpress.com

This book is written with the constant blessing of my parents

Mr. Anil Rai Samsuhang

Mrs Sunita Rai Samsuhang

The poems are dedicated to thousands of souls that passed away during the pandemic.

And is completed in memory of my mentor

Late Dr. Dick. B Dewan

MA, MED, MPhil, PhD

Contents

Preface

The book in hand is an endeavoring work of the author and has come to existence with constant strife. The book is a collection of my poems written with great enthusiasm and thinking. The lyrics are lucid and enjoyable. The genre of writing focuses on nature, life, sorrow, love, and education. My strong interest and love for my writing of mine have made this work complete. As a student, I was able to manage time for writing poems and fulfill my desire for a fickle mind. There was no day that passed without paper and pencil, indeed without a poem. I composed these works when I felt the serenity of life and had a jovial mind. Anything that you do gets great when you are relaxed and happy, and mine result is the book which you are holding. I too have invested an equal amount of time in the competition of the anthology. My pure dedication made it easier throughout this journey of writing. Some of my poems really show a deep sense of feelings, felt by each person on earth.

'A good thing about writing is you can write anything.'

~ Anmol Rai Samsuhang

I have quoted the above sentence and it is so true. I have also waited so long for the publication of this work and perhaps it's one of the best moments ever in my life. This kind of work is sure to come in the upcoming days, with much improvement and perfection. I am very confident that I will continue on the path of literature, and will evolve into a great stature. The feeling of this successful work is a very euphoric one, so I feel grateful that I was able to present my work before you all. Poetry goes so smoothly when you experience nostalgia, sorrow, and harshness. Few of my works express the above feelings. As a young writer I would like to leave a message that you can achieve anything at the present moment, there is no specific age for doing new and exceptional things. I want to thank you all for helping this book to be in your hands, so please enjoy reading!

Anmol Rai Samsuhang

1st January 2023

Acknowledgements

I would firstly like to express my gratitude for those who helped me in the writing and publication of this book. And I am very thankful to everyone for wishing me well and showering abundance of grace. I thank with my folded hands and lowered head to the publishers and editor of this book. I am also grateful to everyone who encouraged me while proceeding to the goal, a great thanks to my holy parents for supporting me through this journey of writing.

I promise everyone that my future works will come to existence with more values, betterment and improvement. To my teachers, I bow my head for providing me the fruitful knowledge and making me to this level. Special thanks to my mentor Late Dr Dick B Dewan from depth of my heart for all educational showering, which he felled upon me.

~Anmol Samsuhang

Introduction

In our daily day to day anecdote, we experience different feeling that mould our body and soul according to the nature of it. Whenever a writer writes something, someway or the other it is related to feelings, either it is imagined or felt.

A poetry is the transformed form of feelings laid by a poet, produced from the connection of the heart and the mind. The nerve impulses which circulate through the neurone is similar with ink being flown into a piece of paper. 'Ink Of Feelings'- the title of the book gives us the sense of feelings embedded within our surroundings which we see daily but can't decipher the true meaning. Every poem here gives you the perception of mixed feelings, perhaps if felt by each one of us on this planet.

My poems also try to convey that things have been started to change drastically with this modernizing world. We have forgotten the things which were once our storehouse of happiness.

In my first poem 'Books are there' readers can find that the cell phones have occupied the fondling love of humans which long ago belonged to books.

Above all these poems are part of my life which I have heard, seen, felt and lived. These are my pieces of life's part, converted to literary figures and sentences. Every time I open to the pages of these poems, I become nostalgic and find myself with a burning zeal of again writing poems with flowing ink of feelings.

ENJOY READING

The author

1. Poems related to education

BOOKS ARE THERE

They are there, seated in the library

Hoping someone to come and relive the moments they have.

They are there, piled up in a shop

Waiting for someone, some inquisitive.

They are there, inside a scholar's bag

Hoping for a new chapter to be opened.

They are there, performing religious rites

Enchanting holy praises.

There are there, seated in the library, for generations

Dusted and become old senile.

They are there, inside a garbage bag

Being thrown away.

They are there, in your room, seeking the place

Where your phone is, elated to get fondle in place of a mobile.

They are there, always there

You just need to reach them to summon

Education

Education is the light to make the future bright
Requiring lots of nights.
Education is the destroyer of evil, a holy fire
It is the way to love life and admire it.
Education is the sea of wisdom
Where ships of knowledge are at freedom.
Education is musical notes of life
Where instruments of minds are at their strife.
Education is the construction of a strong personality
And the foundation of great ability.
Education is the cultivation of a great mind
And the fertilizer for knowledge that binds.
Education is the pilgrimage of thinking
And the devotion to our learning.
Education is great for those who love education
And is the way to success, for those who give dedication.

My classroom Window

My classroom window,
When I sit and take a glimpse,
When the periods are off.
I stare at the towering trees and
Look at the hovering leaves.
I lean on the window sill,
With solitary being filled.
Knowledge is my search,

But every time I get distracted
By the bird that gets parched.
The trees that tower
Makes the leaves shower.
The hills that stood,
Lights up my mood.
The winds snap me out of fatigue,
And brings me back to my body.
As my mind was over the horizon,
Napping in the cotton of clouds.
After all, I find myself,
Sitting near my classroom window.

Scientists

Scientists are the angels with the white coat,
saving the world from pandemics and epidemics.
Embroiling for the betterment,
and experiencing a lot of acrimonies.
From studying the smallest atom to the largest cosmos,
endeavoring in the microscope and
rampaging through the wilderness.
Itemizing with a hypothesis,
and rectifying with experiments.
Handling the delicate living organs,
and mastering the parts of machinery.
Some think mathematically,

to work out the mind.
Some work physiologically,
to save a life, miraculously.
Scientists the people with congenial thoughts,
Strife for the solution until its sought.
Scientists are the helpers who help
The people to understand,
and let the knowledge fill the mind.

Afternoon class

The clock struck one!
the mind shut down.
Boredom-filled
sleepiness build.
Heads get sleepy,
resting on the desk.
My eyes get weepy,
thinking books are pests.
The world seems dreamy
with only the teacher's voice.
Sleep feels creamy
If learning is my choice.
Blackboard moves near
The teacher looks two.
Students are throwing tears,
when the bell goes off,

everyone will cheer.

Minds for the battle

• 5 •

Jotting and mugging,
the lengthy lesson, which is like
preparation for war.
I feel it's coming to me,
bringing a lot of opportunities
and challenges packed together.
The one faced with harshness,
is the one who deserves more success.
It's like climbing a peak, was
thousands of mountaineers trying them
potential by falling and climbing again.
Aiming for the greatest and sacrificing all their wealth
for a single position to be occupied.
Sleepless nights, endless work, and overflowing
tears are the greatest teacher,
which makes these minds for the battle.

2. Poems of nature

Countryside thoughts

In the lap of nature, I take birth
Over the horizon in the earth.
Play messy with soil and dirt
Drink the tasty milk and curd.
Work as a shepherd with the herd
Dance like Michael with the mockingbird.
Gulp the apples of the yard
Now newton lost his word.
Take the fresh air in the head
To get up early from bed,
And not to work as the sleepy head.
When the morning sun shines up
Get to work at the farming plot.
After the sweaty work is done
It's really time for fun.
Traditional folk song is sung
Instruments beating ding, dang, dong.
Then the tasty food is served
With seasoning of the herb.
The wind is becoming fickle

To make the mighty mountains tickle.
The crystal-clear water is flown
All the pollutants are to be thrown.
The wind is staggering in her own
All the negativity is to be blown.
I wail to the birds that fly
In return, they bid me with their melodious cry.
My voice gets through the mountain,
which is covered with clouds of curtains.
The love of mother nature will be sought
If you have countryside thoughts.

A Walk through the hamlet

A walk through the hamlet
Crossing forests, rivers, creeks, and valleys.
Through the lush nature
Where greenery lies and happiness flies.
The houses stood far from each other,
As a reason, no one could bother.
People are jovial carrying everlasting smiles
Closeness with nature and free of poignant feelings.
Working place is a plot, where toiling is a lot
Farming is main if money is to be gained.
The fragrance of the crop is flown, as the wind makes it blown.
Workers dance in the fields, with happiness, overwhelmed.

Life is great there, as the nature care
Living here is easy if you could dare.
A walk through the hamlet turned into
A walk through the realism of life……

Seasons

Seasons come and go
Changing the feelings but the place is the same.
The perception is found while sauntering in the Lane,
Leaves cover the lane and snow stacks the plain.
Fragrance float in the air and the sun shine at the glare.
The bench in the park gets frosted, washed, heated
And blow, but it remains the same.
The outfit of the people changes but the body is the same.
Autumn comes making the trees naked,
And filling the ground with dead leaves.
Spring comes making the flowers bloom,
Welcoming colorful butterflies.
Summer comes making the air warm,
Profiting ice cream sellers.
Monsoon comes making water ample,
And creating zoos of umbrellas.
Winter comes making the place frozen,
Blowing cold breeze into the hot cup of coffee.
Seasons come and goes,
Bringing the change and leaving the joy.

Seasons come and go…

Morning nuance

Early to rise lets you,
feel the real nature.
The truth was concealed
by human pollutants.
Cold fresh air to breathe,
free of poignant feelings.
Tiny dews resting on the
green leaves of the plants,
And golden sunrays falling on them
making them shine like Emerald.
The mighty mountain stood,
followed by the rays falling on them
Making it a gargantuan pile of gold.
The birds chirp and hover, happily
which makes me feel euphoric.
Trees stood high with golden rays on top
flowers start to bloom in the aura that shines.
The sky is magnificently blue azure,
and clouds seem like porpoises in the ocean.
One finds this morning's nuance
If one is early to bed and early to rise.

Woodland time

Into the woods,
into the wilderness.
Through the greenery,
looking at the scenery.
Where giant trees stood,
and animals seeking food.
The floor is dark and cold
as the branches cover all.
The surrounding filled with solitude,
but nature is showing some gratitude.
Birds chirping in distance,
pleasure rising intense.
Hundreds of trees are erected,
maybe god directed.
The leaves float in the gust,
as the trees changed them just.
Giant lying mossy bark,
above there, is a stay of a lark.
I love it so much, this woodland time
when the bugs start to chime.

Evening vibes

I walk through the valley,
during sunset

looking at the hills and the sun meet.
The birds fly over my head
with their family and friends,
as the wilderness calls them home.
The rays of the sun scattered everywhere,
making hundreds of paths.
The sun goes away biding everyone bye
and taking a shift with the moon.
The stars start to reveal them
and begins to twinkle.
The day has gone past,
Night has spread its dark blanket
So, I strolled back to my home,
Carrying these evening vibes.

Lessons from the nature

Like the sun's rays,
squeezing through the spaces
of the dark clouds.
I try to pass through the obstacles
arising along my path.
Like the mountains,
that stood still
during the strongest gust.
I try to remain
fixed at my place

no matter what happens.
Like the water,
changing its shape.
I try to,
mold and adapt
to the situation.
Like the wind spread,
Itself to the whole atmosphere.
I try to expand my knowledge,
to the fullest I can.

Living in harmony

Every morning,
These sparrows and tits
come to my balcony,
to feed upon the moths
attracted by the bulb
during night.
I see two different races
living in harmony and
eating together like a single family.
They possess no fear of me,
one of those look at me suspiciously
and again, continues its work.
So, if birds can live in harmony
why can't we?

Like one family
with no fear of the world.

Hamlets in faraway land

From the greenery that lies
in our place,
and happiness that flies
in our faces.
Jostling rays of sun on the forest and
hurdling flock of arbitrary birds.
Elusive species showing their vibrant, structure
at amidst the wilderness.
Farmers in the heath, doing the
perspiring work, for the good yield for the year.
Lethargic bodies returning from the work
during the meeting of the sun and the mountain.
I keep wondering, glazing at those
hamlets in a faraway land, and
feeling the serenity of the place within my heart.

Countryside road

From the midst of the city cabs,
I mount in the vehicle taking me back home.
I feel intense happiness
when I am able to sense the countryside dust.

I bid on the towering buildings
and people on the street.
I leave the gentle smooth road and
noisy environment.
Now as I reach the countryside road,
Trees welcome me and
workers at the field wave to me.
And I enter the rugged road,
which makes me feel I am at home.
Now I feel I don't need 24 hours electricity,
I need 12 hours of light from the sun rays
which provides me warmth all day long.
I don't need the best-served dishes,
I just need the fresh-grown vegetables
from my garden.
No matter how the situation is,
no matter where I go
my heart will always be in the countryside.

Farmer

On a barren plot,
He is working with sweat and blood
In the scorching heat of the summer sun.
Plowing and tilling the
Same soil year after year.
Senility has touched him,

And his body needs rest
But to fill the empty stomachs
He has no excuses to make
This is called true love, I thought
Though he owned a barren land,
He never had a barren hope.

Withered roses

Oh! These withered roses,
Which were once the
Attractions for all.
As I asked it, that how did you end up here
It said, I feel blessed to die here in my house,
I didn't have to go to the hand of some lovers,
I didn't have to be on the burial of a deceased man,
I didn't have to be on the bouquet with another flower,
So, I feel blessed dying here.
Although one of the flowers was dead,
The plant had not lost its hope.
It bearded numerous buds
over its body.
Waiting until the time comes and
It can show up the world as new fresh roses.

3. Poems of life

Life

What is life? Exclaimed an old man
His mind traveled like a time machine,
Recapitulating everything.
A woman gives birth to a child,
The child gets fondled in her lap.
Grows up with his father
Seeks knowledge as a scholar
Starts to live life as a bachelor.
He murmured… Life is a journey
Finds his partner for life
Gets married and makes her wife
Both continue to strife.
It's a jovial journey! He shrieked
Life is inherent, consonant with God
Some die early, some die late
Some peacefully, some dreadfully
some as infants, some as centenarians.
Hopefully, I am an octogenarian…. He spoke
Earnestly he interrogated himself
What if I die? He whimpered

If I die, I will rest in nature

My name will be forgotten in nature

My spirit will elude in nature

My body will decrease in nature

He infirmly said ''this is life'' and breathed his last……

Centenarian

I met a centenarian

Sitting on a bench

Her face frowned

Her body was infirm

She was dressed in a traditional attire

I bowed to

And she smiled with the blessing

Her hand was wrinkled

Full of feebleness

She held a wooden walking stick

And prayer beds on the other

She talked to me, with her stammering

And shaking voice

I answered with respect

Absorbing her golden pieces of advice

I look into her white, senile eyes

Where there is more hope to go…….

Nightmare

A tall slender woman always comes
When I am asleep
She mysteriously comes and goes
Circling my bed numerous times
She wears a dark old robe
And her head is bald
She murmurs some dark enchantment
From her old leather book,
Very difficult to decipher
She stood at the window
Looking at sky
Looking for the moon to come
And when the moon has shown
She laughs vulgarly
Making my room thunderous
Her bony hand held a crystal knife
Staggering towards me
She utters something, holding the knife
Aiming at me
My spirit left no place, my body was
Sweaty under the cover of my blanket
She poked my belly! Ouch! Aha!
I snapped out of confusion
Revealing it was a nightmare……

Eternal

Eternal is my love,
immortal is my care.
We are like those doves
living for each other, with an alluring dare.
Eternal is our match,
that none can detach.
And so is our love, that never dies
our heart is like birds, that together fly.
Eternal is our relationship,
that is regard to God we worship.
You and I are the ascetics
looking for truth and are on a pilgrimage of love.
Eternal is our walk,
That never stops and has no end.
Peaceful is the journey with loveable talks.
Jovial is our life that none can bend.

Gloomy are the days

Gloomy are the days,
sorrow is my mind.
Solitude is my place
tears is that bind.

Broken is my heart,
taken is my soul.
Sadness increases in my chart,
loneliness makes me growl.
Fickle are the thoughts,
benumbed is my body.
Decision are the worst,
I am fully lost.
Gloomy are the days,
Gloomy is the past
Gloomy is my heart
And gloomy is me, gloomy is me.
The days gone
The days gone, are passed days
none can be done; nothing can be changed.
Only can be felt and thought,
some makes you laugh and takes your laugh.
The gone days became only a memory,
which I can think and become nostalgic.
People leave this world, leaving behind
the traces of love and sorrow.
The lugubrious moments which
are paradigms of these sorrow.
But gone are gone with the winter's chill
gone with those autumn leaves.
The grim memoirs of the sinful life
and the pious works leaving behind.

Deaden with the memories that
slowly dies too at amidst past and present.

4. Other poems

India

To the glorious golden past to
the swiftly developing present.
I bow to your greatness, my motherland
with all the divinity shown.
Water on three sides,
Desert on the west.
Mountains to the north
and plateaus to the south.
Oh! Great India, you carry billions of heavenly souls.
You gave birth to the greatest of all,
who fought bravely and we did not fall.
Land of Rishi Munis, the storehouse of knowledge
and teacher of the world.
Different cultures
grow and spread,
with the oldest civilization lived.
Ancient structures you have,
and greatest technology you had.
Holy celestial Ganges that
distribute the divinity along.

Animals love to reside,
without any fear at all.
Even gods laid their feet in you, and
With this, we can know how great you are.
I LOVE YOU INDIA
BANDE MATARAM

Where you've been?

Where you've been? my friend
I've been to the playground down,
But ran away after I saw a clown.
Where you've been? my brother
I've been to the gym,
Got a little sweaty, but now I got to swim.
Where you've been? my sister
I've been to the saloon
And have brought party balloons.
Where you've been? mother
I've been to the market,
Where I lost my locket.
Where you've been? father
I've been to the bank,
Where I saw a man like a tank.
Where you've been? Anmol
Oh! I've been writing a poem,
Wait! My papers are being blown.

Love for Kolakham

Like lucidity in my dreams,
this is kolakham, that I've seen
Like cold water flowing in the stream,
To the majestic Chhagay falls I've been.
Gargantuan hills of Neora, Lava and Rishop covers me,
I look at myself as manikin as I see.
Like a forum for animals that graze,
and feels heaven when the mighty Kanchenjunga raise.
Penultimate region of joshmani sects,
And the divinity of Baudha Dham awaits.
Shimmering morning rays light up the mood,
And the rosy flow of vegetarian food.
Like a lucidity in my dream,
This is kolakham, where I was born.

Streets of Kalimpong

The streets of Kalimpong, with busy pedestrians
walking everywhere, are scattered in the smallest space.
Jostling each other to get to the respective destination.
Some with loads and bags, returning from the weekly market.
Vendors and shopkeepers toil to their most,
for attracting the walking bodies.
Children with tantrums for the new locked stuff.

Air filled with the fragrance of delicious food,
and heart filled with the love of Kalimpong.
Bloggers, blogging for their channel growth,
and musicians, playing the melody for the box to be filled.
Students with the tidy dresses seek the
way to school in those busy areas.
Cops controlling the traffic with
their sharp whistle.
And fast-food sellers distribute
hot cooked meals to the customers.
At the end of the, I return from where I came,
through these streets of Kalimpong.

The room full of corpse

In the camps of Auschwitz
where those who stepped, were
crushed, bruised, and killed.
People with dead bodies
fighting the dreadful sepsis.
And children with hopeful dreams
to live their future bright.
But gone are those dreams,
in the room full of corpse
where gas chambers were built for the massacre
of those innocent beings.
Unholy is the hearts of the badge bearers,

who put the uniform to kill
those sprouting souls.
The room full of corpses, with
the souls full of sorrow.

The silent night

The silent night, and the silent streets
through which I walk.
My soul gets in solitude,
feeling the loneliness and silence.
The darkness which I face,
makes my body go for a race.
I think of the dark patches and the
black shadows casting a spell on me.
The dogs howling, and cats purring
makes me gingerly stroll in the lane.
When my steeps rake,
the noise is great.
The smallest quake, I can sense
The dripping water, the clicking clock
and my confused heart.
As I was walking in the silent night.

Along the Teesta

Along the Teesta,

I move
Glazing to its magnificence
And realizing its significance.
Along the Teesta,
I move
Bowing to its holiness
And praising its greatness.
Along the Teesta,
I move
Thinking of its blue-green water
And the absence of a single litter.
Along the Teesta,
I move
Walking along with it
And also taking a rest a bit.

Stray dog

I found a stray dog,
Penetrating in a dustbin.
Looking for some food,
To drive away the hunger.
When it came out with nothing,
Its eyes caught me.
Flickering it's tail
And rushing towards me.
With the hope of some love,

It followed me through the lane.
My heart showed compassion,
Telling me to fondle it.
I turned back and
Walked close it,
Filled with some fear, it hesitated.
Although, after I touched it
It got calm, and became full of trust.
I found a stray dog
But now, no more a stay.

The old mansion

The old mansion lies
In the middle of the forest.
With a gigantic brown roof,
And a massive entrance.
Darkness covers the wide halls,
And cobwebs surround the stairways.
Dust fills the ground,
Smell flows in the air.
Walls bear old portrait
With memories trapped in them
Furniture of antiquity,
With vintage architecture.
Ambiance with phobias
And nuance of fear.

The old mansion, always
Stand in the wilderness.